Secrets to a Successful Online Romance

By

Jensel Darul

authorHOUSE

1663 Liberty Drive, Suite 200
Bloomington, Indiana 47403
(800) 839-8640
www.authorhouse.com

First published by AuthorHouse 05/31/04

ISBN: 1-4184-3115-X (e)
ISBN: 1-4184-3116-8 (sc)

This book is printed on acid-free paper.

Table of Contents

INTRODUCTION

Do you know how many people there are in the world looking for that special someone who will brighten up their day?

Just make a search on any Search Engine or visit any of the Personals Channels or Directories found on so many websites or visit the Chatrooms when you are online and you will come across males looking for females and vice versa. With their ages ranging from 18 years onwards, these Net users are looking for new friends, casual dates and/or even true love. They are looking for their match, their soul-mate.

For the greenhorn on the Net, BEWARE! The human beings on the Net are not always honest! They may not be single and available - even if they portray themselves to be so. Many are already hitched and live with their spouses and children. But that lifelong commitment of 'Till death do us part' has not stopped their quest for …..
… the mysterious,
… the unknown,
… the untried and
… the undiscovered to spice up their lives.

Yes, if you have a computer and have access to the World Wide Web, you are spoilt for choice where making friends is concerned because you can make friends with people from all over the world: from Afghanistan to Zimbabwe. They will be from all walks of life, ranging from a caravan owner to a computer scientist.

You could also find people with the most unusual hobby because the hobbies of Net users from around the world could range from cacti growing to yoga and meditation. On the Net, although the majority of Net users communicate in English, you may be able to find some who speak and communicate in languages ranging from Abkhazian to Zulu.

Why are there so many people searching on the Net? In today's world, fewer and fewer people are living in communities or the extended family system where there is constant interpersonal communication. Many live in nuclear families. Some live on their own, away from their homes and family because of their studies or their jobs. Many more choose to live single lives so that they are not tied down by the demands of nurturing a family.

Since humankind is a social being that needs to communicate, many people spend time online looking for company: someone to talk to and share the different aspects of their lives with, the joys and sorrows, the ups and downs, the good and the bad. They are looking for a virtual friend and companion.

In this age of modern technology, you need not have to sit at the local café to mingle and get to know people. You can go online and get a host of friends who will exchange e-mail messages with you and also spend hours chatting. This will be done in the comfort of your home or anywhere else where you are most relaxed and have Internet access.

When the atmosphere is conducive, you will begin to enjoy the online relationship, be it a friendship or a romance. Through this faceless human interaction online, we form relationships, not based on the physical characteristics like the muscular physique of a male or the captivating figure of a female. The formation of these online relationships is based on the meeting of minds.

Participating in online relationships has many benefits. If these relationships grow positively and are nurtured well, off-line relationships may also improve. Besides, you will be richer because of the experiences that you share with one another since in getting to know someone, you will be exchanging news and views, maybe even getting a different perspective of life and definitely getting added knowledge about different cultures and traditions. It could be an experience so very different from your normal mundane day-to-day living.

The irony about reaching out to others is that in communicating with others, you are getting involved in the process of self-discovery. How does self-discovery take place? Sometimes, it is because when you are asked questions about yourself which you had previously taken for granted, you have to search your soul for the answers, the reasons and the explanations. Sometimes in discussing life's issues, you will learn where your priorities lie, what is important to you, what your goals in life are and where you are heading.

Researchers say that online relationships have a limited lifespan. Just like friends in the real world, online friends come and go. There will be times when they will send you messages everyday. And yet there will be occasions when you do not hear from them for days on end.

If you wish to nurture your online friendship so that your friend does not get lost in the virtual world, but instead the friendship blooms into an online romance, then this book is for you. The different issues involved in an online romance are told from a female perspective.

CHAPTER 1

FRIENDSHIP OR ROMANCE

Online friends can be made 24/7, but are you interested in an online romance? A romance sounds more intriguing, doesn't it?

Every romance should begin with being friends. If you find that you feel so comfortable with him that you want to make it a little more special, you could then continue that lovely relationship with that 'special someone' to make it into a loving relationship.

That 'special someone' could be miles and miles away. You might have never known the existence of him, but because of the innovations in modern technology, you have met virtually and now you feel you have been given a chance to express your feelings of love, even though you have never seen his face or heard his voice.

An online romance could also be with your next-door neighbour whom you are too shy to speak to face-to-face. It could be with the stranger you met while on your way to work whom you know you may never meet again, but who you feel would be so very nice to get to know in a very special way now that you have exchanged e-mail addresses.

So do you have someone in mind whom you would like to have an online romance with? Does the name of the latest TV heartthrob come to mind? If you can get his/her e-mail address, what is there to stop you from trying? Nothing ventured, nothing gained!

An online romance is different from online dating. In online dating you are communicating with the other because you want to get to know him better. In an online romance, you have already got to know him. You are friends and now you want to proceed on to the next level of friendship – to share a romance.

Romance – the expressions of love between couples – plays an important role in today's relationships. The period of time for romance varies from couple to couple. Some couples share a romantic relationship throughout their time together. Some couples share romantic moments in fits and starts.

Many couples are not so lucky. They may have never experienced romance in their lives. This is because some relationships have been and are very mechanical: if one party finds that they get along well with the other, the next course of action would be to settle down and start a family.

Culture and the strict conventions of society could have hindered the process of romance, for example, in arranged marriages. In these situations, couples would have missed out on romance before the marriage. Romance could blossom after the marriage but with the babies coming along and eking out a living, romance is often sidelined.

Before you take the first step into an online romance, you must ask yourself why you are doing it and whether you will be able to handle it.

CHAPTER 2

WHY AN ONLINE ROMANCE?

We are living in the age of technology where just about everything can be done using computers, from shopping to getting a degree. It is not surprising then that the computer-savvy use the Net to find friends and even romance.

The Reasons

There are many reasons why Net users go for online romances. Here are some of them:

"It is exciting. It is mysterious even, since my best friend doesn't know that I am having an illicit relationship with someone online."

"It takes me away from the real world of daily chores of looking after my two kids and cooking for my husband."

"My wife has no time for me. She is always busy with the children and her work. I need this outlet. I need to chat with someone about religious beliefs, work, television programmes and anything else under the sun"

"In a way, it is safe because my online friend is thousands of miles away. I know I will not be harassed."

"It saves me the hassle of having to impress my date every time. Online, I spend so much less and most of the time the cost is shared. Because of that, we meet more often too."

"I don't have to bother about dressing up or getting caught in traffic – all the inconveniences I need to go through just to spend time with someone I like."

"He is a political figure and he needs to protect his image. What more, he is married! So since we get on well with each other, the best way to carry on as secret lovers is online."

"It is fascinating to know that someone at the other end of the computer is thinking of me and has that special feeling for me."

"There has been a difference in me. I feel like a better person and so I treat my family members in a better way. I don't feel so grouchy."

"Every time I receive a message from my online girlfriend, it gives me a special lift for the day."

"I have found a true friend, someone with whom I can discuss my wishes, hopes, beliefs and dreams on a regular basis. Also I can share all my frustrations, fears and disappointments with her. She is my virtual angel."

"On the Net, I can remain anonymous if I so wish. I like doing that at the start of the relationship. I only reveal my true self when I am sure that the other can be trusted. In real life, that is hard to do."

"I do not feel inhibited online. I can say whatever I want and whatever I feel."

"I don't have to worry about interferences from other parties, like well-meaning friends and relatives. When I am ready and my romance partner is ready, we will reveal our little secret to the world… but until then, it remains a secret only between the two of us."

"In real-life relationships, we tend to dismiss certain things which are said. We only look for the non-verbal cues. At most times, we do not listen well enough to the words. In sending e-mail and chatting, nothing is lost.

I normally read every single message that he has written, sometimes more than once, to get at the underlying meaning and the feelings involved. Yes, I really analyse him through his words."

"I was forced to marry my uncle. It was an arranged marriage and more a marriage of convenience. I feel I have missed out on romance. I feel jealous when my friends talk about their romantic moments. I want to experience it too. Online seems to be the only way, so that my husband won't find out."

"While enjoying the online romance, I can still carry on with my daily living. I do not have to give up anything. I have the freedom to do what I want, when I want. I am still independent. I don't feel tied down by the demands that are normally associated with a romance."

.

.

.

.

And the list goes on.

Romance means that besides just being friends, you have that special feeling between two persons that cannot be expressed in words. And get ready for this!

The beauty about having an online romance is that it comes with no strings attached, unless you want them to be attached. It is unconditional. You will have no prying eyes or wagging tongues probing into your love life to find out how the relationship is going.

In fact, no one needs to know your 'little secret', unless you want them to know about it. There is no pressure from any party to insist that you 'do the right thing and get married since you have been seeing each other for so long and it is time you settled down.'

An online romance involves positive mutual feelings between two human beings who feel so much for each other that they decide it must have been a miracle to have found the other since there are nearly a billion Net users.

An online romance sounds so tempting! So romantic! So exciting! However, a friendship will not become a romance overnight. So, just as in a real life situation, if an online romance is your goal, you must work at it to make it happen.

Can you handle the romance?

Do you want to be involved in an online romance? Or do you think that the two of you should just remain friends? Are you ready for it?

Many sceptics say that an online romance encourages one to live in a fantasy world. They say that it is not a real relationship. With today's advances in information communication and technology, one can make it as real as one wants it to be, no matter what the physical distance between the two parties involved are. The world is now considered a global village so if both parties agree, an online romance can always take them to the next level of a relationship - a lifelong commitment in the institution of marriage.

The choice on how you deal with the online relationship and what direction you wish it to take depends on the parties involved. You could share your deepest secrets and most intimate moments with the soul mate you have found in cyberspace or you could just keep it casual and still share romantic feelings.

There is one major drawback in an online romance, though. In cyberspace, you will have to deal without the physical presence. Can you deal with the reality that the five senses are absent in the relationship? There is no seeing, hearing, touching, smelling or tasting.

Don't lose heart, though! All is not lost. The sixth sense (what some people call intuition), the gut feeling, may become more prominent as the relationship develops. With the special intimacy you share, you will be able to feel the hugs and kisses, even without any physical contact. Only time and your 'sense' of the other will tell. This would also differ from one couple to the next.

Undeniably, the absence of the physical has its benefits. As in a real-life relationship, in the online romance, you have to some day decide where to draw the line concerning sexual intimacy. In your online communication, you will never need to feel physically outraged and sexually harassed to shout RAPE. When things get out of hand, all you need to do is to cut off the electronic communication and decide whether you want to get connected again or just end the relationship.

Yes, you cannot touch each other, you cannot hold, you cannot be together, but you can share sweet and tender moments. As the relationship progresses, you will become bolder in telling the secrets you would not share with anyone in your physical surroundings. These personal 'sharings' will eventually lead you both to feeling a sense of oneness and togetherness.

This kind of sharing has been therapeutic for many. The parties involved in this kind of relationship normally begin to feel a certain sense of self-worth because there is someone there to listen to them. It is definitely not unhealthy. If the relationship is nurtured well, you will realise that it has reached that particular stage not because of any physical attraction but because of the meeting of souls and minds.

Can you imagine the heights you could take the online relationship to? When you are online at your computer communicating with your potential romance partner, he is also at his technological tool giving you his full attention. It is similar to one soul talking to another soul. There would normally be no interferences and no outside distractions. Depending on how much of yourself you reveal to him, it is in this kind of atmosphere that the feeling of intimacy leading to romance will be nurtured.

Have you been tempted into wanting to start an online romance so far? It is not as easy as it seems because despite the vast number of Net users throughout the world, it is very difficult to find someone whom you can 'click' with, someone who will have the same goals as you, someone who has the same interests as you and someone who inspires love in you.

Don't despair! Thirty years ago, the majority of people communicated with others around a 50 km radius of their place of work or home. If you go online today, the world is your oyster! The miracle about modern day technology is that you can take advantage of the Internet and start up a friendship with anyone, even someone who is living on the opposite side of the world. Out of all the many friends you have online, there will definitely be someone whom you want to be romantic with, and vice versa.

So are you ready to take up the challenge? If so, where will you meet and how will you communicate?

CHAPTER 3

THE MAIN VEHICLES

There are many channels by which one person can communicate with another person these days, if there is no face-to-face communication. Besides talking over the telephone, one can also send SMS (short messaging service) messages. Online, one can have net meetings and videoconferencing.

However, for that special one-to-one communication online, the two most common ways of communicating today are by sending e-mail messages and by chatting.

i) E-mailing

You can instantly send and receive electronic mail (e-mail) from around the world if you have an e-mail software programme. The friend whom you communicate with by sending e-mail messages is your keypal, e-friend or e-pal. In this book, we will refer to your online friend as your e-pal.

Having an e-pal is similar to having a pen-pal, except that online, the correspondence is faster, cheaper, more convenient and more informal. It saves you the hassle of standing in line at the Post Office to find out the postage of any letter or card you want to send by snail mail to someone living in another country.

Because you can e-mail from the comfort of your home, you can do it at any time you want, day or night, and as many times a day (or night) as you want. If you are 'crazy in love' and keep sending messages every minute, your e-pal will be deluged with mail when he goes to his In-box to retrieve his mail. If the tables are turned and you are the one receiving the deluge of mail, won't you feel you are walking on cloud nine the whole day?

If you feel that you can express yourself well in the written word, then having an e-pal will be very rewarding. Like all forms of communication, the formality of the message depends on how you perceive yourself, how you perceive the other person and the message you want to convey.

When putting your thoughts into words, you should always bear in mind that what you write and how you say it will create an impression of you in the mind of the person who reads it. So, when you write a message, you should always ask yourself: What kind of impression do I want to leave on my e-pal's mind?

Writing to the e-pal of your prospective online romance would be informal. This is because you are one step ahead of a normal friendship. You have passed that hurdle. You have broken the ice, have felt a special liking for the person you have been corresponding with and are now taking the relationship to the next level.

The informality of the messages may take different forms. Both of you may be so familiar with each other that you might even have your own lingo. Familiarity is also shown when the e-mail message begins without a salutation like "Hello" or "Dear …." or ends without a complimentary close like "Yours" or "Sincerely". This is a sign that the other finds you so comfortable to write to that he can do away with the conventions of letter writing. It is made possible by the fact that you write to each other often.

The effect of reading informal messages received through snail mail and e-mail is totally different. Imagine how you would feel if your pen pal writes you a letter which has no salutation or complimentary close. You would definitely feel insulted! But you will feel more relaxed with the relationship if this happens in the e-mail messages.

Writing in a conversational manner in an e-mail will put both of you at ease. It is therefore not necessary to crack your head over a subject heading. In fact, since all e-mail messages should have a subject heading, you could start your message at the subject heading itself. The following e-mail message is an example.

Subject: I really ……

…. enjoyed the time we spent chatting yesterday. I got to know you better, and I loved the way you used all the emoticons to show your reaction towards my comments.

You have a great sense of humour and I really enjoy chatting with you.

When are you free for another chat? Let's make it this weekend.

Your Special Someone.

It is good to write short paragraphs with a space in between paragraphs for easy reading. Correct punctuation, grammatically correct sentences and correct vocabulary show the extent to which you respect the person who is receiving the message. It can also prevent a lot of misunderstanding due to misinterpretation of the message.

As the relationship becomes even less formal, sending a message of one paragraph is acceptable. Writing just a sentence or even a question is common. In fact, sometimes even a word or a phrase will suffice.

If your e-pal has not sent you a message in a while, you could send him a blank e-mail with the subject heading 'Why no mail?' Put it in block letters for a greater dramatic effect as shown.

You would never dream of sending three words on a blank piece of letter-pad paper by snail mail. It would definitely not be practical to do so!

Care should also be taken with the way you word your message because sometimes the message can be misunderstood. It is very difficult to take back a remark or comment that has been written. Remember that your romance partner may come from another culture totally different from yours, and sometimes even the simplest words can have different connotations.

Let me relate a personal experience about the way words can be misinterpreted because of differences in culture. Once, an e-pal asked me how I felt about him. I said that he was 'nice'. At once his advances lessened. I was surprised as we seemed to be getting on quite well. Later he told me that in his country in the northern hemisphere, saying someone was *nice* meant that you were not interested in him at all. I explained to him that to me and the people living in the tropical region, saying someone was *nice* meant that we felt that the person was good, kind and polite.

So it is important that you have a broad outlook on the world. In this way, you will have a better idea of how the rest of the world perceives certain issues and not be easily offended by the comments of others.

Some Traits of E-mailing

In an e-mail message, you are allowed to do the following as the messages become less formal:

1) You could use more than one exclamation mark or question mark to show surprise or shock.

Whaaaaaatttt!!!! You were sleeping the whole time!!!!!

Did you say that you went to bed at 1a.m. on Friday night? Now, it is 3p.m. Sunday afternoon and you say you did not send me any messages because you were sleeping?????

2) You do not need to follow the conventions of perfect spelling. For example, certain letters in a word could be repeated to show extremes.

You are soooooooooo very thoughtful!

3) Block letters could be used for certain words to show that you are emphasizing them.

I want YOU to tell ME that YOU LOVE ME.

4) However, do not use block letters throughout the message because this means that you are yelling or shouting and so your romance

partner will assume that you are being rude or that you are angry. That will only spoil the romantic mood!

WHAT ARE YOU DOING?

---

5) Refrain from using SMS lingo, for example,
'What R U doing on Sun AM?'
to mean
'What are you doing on Sunday morning?'
unless, of course, the two of you are familiar with the shortened words. If you are not careful, it could get you into trouble. What do you think this message means?

I am having my BF now.

'BF' is commonly associated with boyfriend, but here breakfast is meant. Can you think of other interpretations for 'BF'?

6) Because you can send e-mail messages at any time of the day or night, it is not necessary for them to be lengthy. Keep the message as concise as possible and if you feel like it, make use of the benefits of e-mail technology and send your messages as often as you like. Word each e-mail message differently for better effect.

The Little Secrets

What are the little secrets to starting an online romance through e-mailing and seeing it through for as long as you can?

1) Write as often as you can. This will show that your e-pal is always on your mind. It works to your benefit also because in writing often, you will also ensure that you are always on your e-pal's mind.

2) Reply to any e-mail that you receive as soon as you can. This will show that you are interested, and that you respect him since you do not keep him waiting for a reply. (Once in awhile, though, you could intentionally not reply so that your e-pal will not take you for granted!)

3) Don't write only for a specific reason. Write just to say "Hello". It also means "I have been thinking of you." Do you remember the song 'I just called to say I love you'?

4) Answer all the queries that are asked in an interesting fashion. When you click 'reply' to a message, you will find your e-pal's message. Put in your own comments after each comment that he has made. It would look as if you were having a conversation and you found everything he said worth pondering over and commenting on.

>I don't know what to do this weekend.
We could spend the weekend together chatting or you could take me for a ride on your superbike in cyberspace! Wouldn't that be spectacular?

>I have been working so hard and coming home after 10 every night.
Do have a proper night's sleep and take care of your health. Don't stress yourself up too much. Let's spend some time relaxing together this Friday night.

---

5) Try to get your e-pal involved in the message as well. Notice the way the next message is worded. The writer has skilfully given the impression that her e-pal is much better at handling the situation, thus boosting his ego.

> ....That was what I did when I saw the boy throw the popcorn away. I am sure you would have had a better way of dealing with the situation. What would you have done?

6) Ask questions about issues that are general or global in nature. The replies will help you get to know your e-pal better: his beliefs, his values and his stand on certain issues, maybe even the political party he supports.

7) Whenever in doubt about what has been said, seek clarification.

> What did you mean when you wrote that you really need me?

8) Share with your e-pal aspects of your life that are worthwhile sharing. These should portray you as an interesting and positive-minded person. If you had an e-pal who had nothing interesting to say or write about, but who always grumbled and was sometimes even rude, would you still carry on with the correspondence?

9) Create your own little quirks in your messages – a way of starting your message or a particular way of ending it. The following are examples:

> My Darling Deer
> How have you been?

> Be good and don't do anything I wouldn't do.
>
> Your Special Someone

Today's e-mail software programmes also sometimes allow you to add photos to the message. You could change the background colour and use special stationery and graphics. However, using these will be a waste of time if your e-pal is using a browser system that does not support them.

10) Tell your e-pal what you like about him and why the relationship is still moving along smoothly. Remember to do this regularly. The following are some ways of showing that you appreciate the effort he is putting into the relationship:

I like it when you address me as 'Darling Deer' in all your e-mail messages.

I feel happy when I receive an e-mail message from you, especially since it is the first thing you do when you wake up in the morning.

I would love it if you could send me an e-mail message every night before you go to bed too.

How else would your romance partner know you are happy with the course of events in the relationship if you do not communicate these feelings to him? Remember that he is not around to see that glint in your eye or that nervous look on your face, or experience that excitement when you get mail from him. So the only way he will know that you appreciate him is if you tell him! And remember to do it often!

In short, then, since you have the time to think and compose a reply when sending an e-mail message, make use of this benefit for the progress of the romance. Take time with your message. You can prepare your responses to the messages you have received, review your message at your own leisure and then decide whether you want to send off those messages.

If you are not sure, hold on to the messages. Save the drafts, review and edit them until you are satisfied.

Choose your words correctly. Avoid being impulsive and always see things from the other person's point of view. This will save you from embarrassing situations or situations which you may regret later.

The major benefit of e-mailing is that if you put effort into the process, it will definitely improve your writing skills and your way of expressing yourself in words.

ii) Chatting

There are many chatrooms where you can arrange to meet your e-pal for a webchat and yet not talk out loud. A webchat is an instant real-time conversation in text form. Some chatrooms are provided by Yahoo Messenger, MSN Messenger and ICQ. Many chatrooms come complete with sound, images and even video. So with a webcam today, one can even see the person one is chatting with.

The advantage of chatting is that it is immediate. In chatting, you will have to type in your words in reply to the chat message sent by your chat partner. You cannot keep your chat partner waiting for too long for a reply. It is similar to having a conversation, only that here you are typing out everything that you would have said in a real-life face-to-face communicational situation.

Unlike sending an e-mail message, there is not much time in a chatroom to prepare your responses, but there is a little more time than if you were to speak to the person on the phone or face-to-face. If you chat often then, you will improve your typing or word-processing skills.

You and your chat partner can do lots of things together while chatting. While he is at a conference, with his laptop in front of him, he could be chatting with you. You could be doing your research while he is reading the news online and you could still be chatting.

Or maybe both of you could be studying together in different corners of the world, but while online and via the chat software program, you could pass comments now and then, to encourage each other along. Unlike e-mailing then, when chatting, both of you will be communicating with each other in real time.

Some Traits of Chatting

1) Because it is real-time conversation and you want to get your ideas across as quickly as possible, you may find that you are using the same words or phrases over and over again. Since you are chatting in an informal situation, you can shorten these words and phrases to speed up your typing and the chat session.

Snakeye   : How did U enjoy the annual dinner?
            Were many people present at the AD?
            Was your ex there too?
Jade   : Not bad. There was good food and
            lots of new faces at the AD.

A stranger may wonder what AD is. But Jade and Snakeye know what they are talking about.

2) Sometimes only small letters (no capitals) are used. This is done to speed up the typing. It seems a bit odd but today many chatters are used to the 'i' rather than the 'I' when talking about themselves.

Snakeye   : how did u enjoy the dinner?
Jade   : not bad. i wish u could have been there.

---

3) SMS lingo (or weblish) can be used.

```
Snakeye    : R U sure U don't wanna chat longer?
             Btw, i am off 2morro!
Jade       : i m tired. i need to rest. Mayb 2morro!
```

4) There are also lists of emoticons, abbreviations and lingo which are commonly used by people who regularly chat. (These are discussed in Chapter 5.) These lists can be found on the Net. They help you get your ideas across and speed up your chat session. Alternatively, you could be innovative and come up with your own list, but make sure that your chat partner knows what your short forms mean to avoid misunderstanding.

The Little Secrets

What are the little secrets to going the extra mile in a chat session to nurture that romantic feeling?

1) Make time for a regular chat session. It shows that the relationship is significant to you and that it is worth your time.

2) During the chat session, give your chat partner your whole attention and focus. Make him your first priority. Even if your chat partner is on the other side of the world, he will be able to detect if you are responding wholeheartedly or if you are distracted.

3) Be sensitive to what your chat partner is saying and respond to his comments quickly. Keep in mind that you are communicating with a human being and so you need to be courteous and considerate.

4) Give allowance for the fact that both of you may be from different parts of the world and have had different experiences. So if you have any doubt about what your chat partner has written, do not feel shy to ask for an explanation when something that is said seems uncalled for.

5) Do not let misunderstandings brew. Try to iron out the misconceptions as soon as they are typed out. A reply to a simple question like "What do you mean?" or "I don't understand." can clarify a lot of doubts.

Basically the main secrets of e-mailing would also apply to chatting, since both are vehicles for online communication, except that the former is asynchronous while the latter is synchronous. We should always bear in mind that it is the people who are communicating, not the computers. The computers are only the tools that aid the process of communication.

The chat session is a good avenue to show your care and concern in real-time, because here you are slightly more spontaneous in your responses than in the e-mail messages. Be attentive and ask relevant questions for the relevant occasion. Be tactful by saying the right thing at the right time. This will definitely win you a few points in the mind of your chat partner, who will be able to detect your sincerity by your spontaneity.

If you are distracted by the hundred and one other things that can be done on the Net, tell your partner about it. For example, while chatting, you may come across a website that has humourous e-cards. Tell him that you are at that site. He may visit it too and then that would be a common ground for you to start a discussion, and maybe tease each other about sending the cards to your favourite people.

When you devote quality time to a relationship, the other party will feel valued and will certainly appreciate it. Have you ever been with someone where throughout the time you were together, this person was on the cellular phone deep in conversation with someone else? How did that make you feel?

Everyone likes to feel valued and appreciated. So if you are interested in nurturing that special romantic feeling with your chat partner, make the person feel he is someone important in your life. Use loving words and flirt with him, and enjoy the response that you get.

On the other hand, if your chat partner is of no significance to you and there are no inclinations towards romance, then you can ignore his messages and his requests for chat sessions. The relationship will die a natural death as one person cannot carry on a romance by himself and with himself!

It is expected for people to equate romance with sex. The chat session is a common place for sex-related topics to be discussed. Some chatters can be very daring in their comments in a chat session. If the issue of sex and sexual activities comes up, it is up to you to decide whether you have reached that stage in the relationship and want any part of it. Do not feel obligated. If it is brought up in your first chat session or every time you chat, it can be a big turn off. Remember that one can have good clean romance without any 'sex' involved.

The difference in time zones should also be considered especially when you are planning a chat session. It would be a hindrance to the relationship if both parties cannot find the time to get online for a chat session. Make arrangements by e-mail. Come to a compromise and choose a time that suits the two of you. Once the date is made, make it a point to show up. If you cannot make it, you should have the courtesy to send your apologies by e-mail. Don't keep your chat partner waiting.

One of the greatest benefits of having an online romance through the online vehicles of communication like e-mail and/or chatting is that you get to savour the intimate moments longer.

How is this possible? You could save the e-mail messages and the chat sessions. You could even get them printed out for further perusal. These printed texts of messages and chat sessions can be perused, scrutinised and mulled over for a long time. They could even be published in your memoirs. They will serve as a lasting record of the time spent with someone you had special feelings for.

By the way, telling your romantic partner that you have saved all the messages and even printed the messages informs him how much you really cherish the relationship that the two of you share.

CHAPTER 4

THE INGREDIENTS

If romance is on your agenda, some ingredients must be present to give a sparkle to the relationship. You must know how to get the attention and affection of the other party once you have decided that you are interested so that the feelings you have can be reciprocated. Let us call the other party your romance partner.

1. Mutuality

An online romance does not just involve one party. There must be a mutual agreement to the type of relationship you both wish to have – friendship, dating, romance or intimacy or a combination of these in varying degrees. Over the Net, it is very difficult to lead the other by the nose into something that he did not bargain for. There must be a mutual consensus.

It is only through the meeting of minds that the relationship can turn into a romance, and each party will be responsible for dictating the pace, whether it goes too fast or moves along for months on end with nothing ever transpiring.

If you want an online romance then, you will have to find out if your online friend has the same intentions as you. You will need to put into words what you feel and expect. If you are on the same wavelength, both desiring an online romance, you will connect mentally and emotionally, treasuring the other's words with meaning and feeling.

> How will you present this proposal of romance to your prospective romance partner?

2. Know yourself

Before taking the friendship to the next level, you should know yourself and decide how much of yourself you want to reveal and share with your romance partner. You should explore what it is in the present relationship that you wish to change. The answers will determine how you present yourself to your prospective romance partner.

If it is romance that you are seeking, then you will work towards an intimate rapport and seek to produce positive feelings in your romance partner. In continuing to send e-mail messages and to chat in the chatroom, you will be able to get to know yourself even better: your values, beliefs, goals and aspirations.

> What do you know about yourself now?

3. Honesty

Honesty is essential in all relationships, more so in an online relationship. You would not want to be cheated by your romance partner, would you? So in the same way, you should treat your romance partner with respect. How do you do that? Easy, be truthful.

You would have been warned many times not to be too generous with information over the Net. Only if you have decided that your romance partner can be trusted should you carry on divulging personal information.

Start off by telling him about your real-life situation, whether you are a cobbler or an astronaut, a zookeeper or a philanthropist.

That is very important because in an online relationship you will be sharing your daily activities and if you live in a world of fantasy, pretending to be someone you are not, in the long run, you will be the one who will be at the losing end of the relationship. Remember that ultimately, the truth always prevails!

So if you are married, live with your in-laws, have a loving husband, go for overseas trips every year, share that with your romance partner. Even if you are a workaholic who lives alone and has ambitions of going to the moon, tell it to your romance partner. This is necessary because you need to build a bond. If you practise honesty, with each passing day, your romance partner will reveal more and more of himself to you.

Can you be honest with your romance partner?

---

4. Sharing

For any relationship to grow, you will have to share yourself with the other. You could share your day's activities with your romance partner. Do not give the standard answer that it has been another boring day. Even if it has been unexciting, put in some excitement to show that you find joy in living.

People are generally not interested in the dull and mundane. To make the relationship work, you would need to find out what your romance partner is interested in so that you could discuss these topics. Also, be enthusiastic about what is happening in the life of your romance partner. Find out if you share interests in similar activities like sports, either watching or playing. Discuss these and other issues like religion, entertainment and hobbies.

After getting to know your romance partner better through the discussions, you will also need to share care and concern, love and affection for the other. From impersonal matters, go on to matters that involve the emotions.

How much of yourself are you willing to share?

5. Bonding

Bonding takes time, and it is a result of sharing experiences. The bonding period will vary with different couples. Have you noticed that in some relationships you have, you can talk about all your problems and successes after the first meeting, and yet in others, you clam up even after being friends for years?

So, if you do not bond on the first instance, do not worry about it. Give it time. Create that bond by discussing situations, historical and current events, local and international news and anything else under the sun.

Before you can bond, you must know what your romance partner values in life and whether you both share the same value system. Logically, the more you differ in your value system, the more likelihood there is that the romance will not last.

Discuss personal matters that you know your romance partner is passionate about. To involve 'feelings' and to create the bond in the relationship, constantly enquire how your romance partner is feeling. At the same time, share your feelings, too. This would work well in a chat session because it takes place in real time.

Do you know your own value system?

6. Trust

Trust is integral to a close bond. If you are honest, your romance partner will learn to trust you. So to instil this trust, you will have to inform your romance partner about what you like and what you do not like. You will have to disclose to him truthfully the way you feel.

You will be surprised at how many of us are not in touch with our feelings. Very often, we come up with stoic responses like "I am doing all right." when someone asks us how we are. But if you can dig deeper with your questioning to find out how your romance partner really feels, he will get a thrill to know that someone really cares to want to know him better and is taking the trouble to find out. This will make him more open to trust you.

How much do you trust your romance partner?

---

7. Deal with Expectations

All too often, when we find ourselves in a relationship that we want to last, we put demands on it. We have our own set expectations and we expect our romance partner to fulfil them. Many a relationship has turned sour because of the unnecessary expectations that are placed on the parties concerned. These expectations are our selfish demands.

We have to learn to deal with expectations and not be too demanding. We should not hope to perform miracles and change our romance partner to suit our desires. Just as we want to have our own space, we should allow our romance partner to grow.

We cannot really have too many expectations in an online romance because you are committed to each other only in the virtual world and so there is no obligation. Thus, if we can train ourselves not to expect too much in an online romance, we will appreciate our romance partner more, especially when he does the unexpected.

> What do you expect from your romance partner?

8. Compromise

In any relationship there has to be give and take. Sometimes, in some relationships, one party gives more than the other. The best way to sort this out is to discuss what we expect in the relationship. How much you give on your part will depend on how much you enjoy the support of the other.

We should not stifle the independence of our romance partner. We should allow him to grow, to experience success and failure, to be his own person, while we are there at the sidelines to lend support.

Yes, it is the complementary aspect of support that nurtures a romantic relationship between couples. As much as you want your romance partner to remember and do what you have told him, on your part you have to always remember what your romance partner has told you, even the smallest detail. Remember that it has to be a two-way interaction.

> Can you compromise or do you always want your way?

9. Be sensitive

When you compromise, you will have to consider your romance partner and his needs. Are you sensitive enough to take the hints and suggestions that she has passed?

What does it mean if she says,

"I do not want a boyfriend who calls once a month."? Could this be a test to see how much you value the relationship? With this broad hint given, what would you then do? Continue to call once a month?

Sometimes you even have to be sensitive to the words that are not said. If you think that you are not sensitive enough to take the suggestions and hints given, ask your romance partner to be more specific and tell you directly what she wants and how you could both work together to make the relationship grow. Then act on it.

> Are you sensitive to the people and situations around you?

10. Seek to Understand

If you want to enjoy the pleasure of having a romance online, you have to know and understand your romance partner. In order to create this understanding, you will need to spend time sharing your feelings in words.

The major drawback about an online romance is that you cannot stare into each other's eyes, hold hands, and walk along the beach or cuddle and pet. What you do really is talk in the printed word. It is through this printed word that you will have to seek to understand your romance partner and what makes him tick. It is in this same way that he will get to know you.

So, do not give one word answers to opinions asked. Elaborate on all your comments, but do not go overboard until your romance partner gets fed up with your long-drawn responses.

> Can you put in words the way you feel?

11. Show Empathy

With understanding comes empathy. Everyone likes someone who can empathise with them – to tell them that they understand what they are going through and support them.

If you value the friendship that you have with your online romance partner, you will not desert him when he is facing difficulties. Instead, you will have to put yourself in his shoes to understand what he is experiencing.

Not everyone will have the gift of putting into words what is experienced. If it is difficult to express everything in words, we have to imagine ourselves in a similar situation. We could ask ourselves what we would have wanted others to do for us if we were in that situation. Then we would know how to react and empathise with our romance partner.

> Are you sensitive enough to be able to empathise with others?

12. Respect

Would you want to start a serious relationship with someone you do not respect? Of course you would not. So to make sure that the romance lasts, you should always have mutual respect for each other.

Because you are in constant communication with your romance partner, you will find yourself telling each other secrets which no one else knows about. In writing, there is a greater tendency of revealing more than in speaking. Respect everything that has been told to you. Keep it confidential. Respect your romance partner's boundaries and privacy.

Do not do anything that will jeopardise your position in the mind of your romance partner. If you find that there is something that your romance partner is avoiding talking about, ask yourself how important it is to you. If it is very important, put it aside for awhile and bring it up at a later date. If it is of no consequence to you, then forget about it. With time, your romance partner may reveal his secrets to you, even without your prodding.

Can you keep a secret?

13. Be sincere

No one likes a person who puts on airs or says things just to get his way. There are many people who pretend to be kind only when they want something in return.

The following message would hold no meaning if it was sent by someone who had not contacted you for months on end. It sounds very insincere!

"When it comes to Valentine's Day, you are the first person on my mind whom I want to send all my love."

On the other hand, if you had been in constant contact, your response to this message would be totally different, I am sure. So if you want to capture the heart of your potential romance partner, you will have to be sincere in your expressions of love at all times, not only when it is convenient to you or on Valentine's Day.

Are you sincere and say only what you feel?

14. Be affectionate

Not everyone is blessed with the same degree of passion and affection. But in order to create that romantic feeling, you can practise using terms of endearment for your romance partner on a regular basis.

'Sweetheart' or 'Huggy bear' are quite endearing. Some have nicknames, for example, 'Jen Jen' for Jennifer. Of course, you should use these terms of endearment only with the consent of your romance partner. You would only be hitting a sore thumb if the terms were not really endearing to your romance partner.

In an online romance, your affections are not displayed with action or emotion. Only words are used to communicate this feeling. However, with the progress in e-mail and chatting, you can also use various emoticons and lingo to express your affection for your romance partner.

> How can you be more affectionate?

15. Be interested

Be interested and show that you are interested. Find out more about the issues that your romance partner is interested in. All you need to do to show your interest are three little words in the e-mail message or chat session:

"Let me know ...."
    or
"Keep me posted."

In this impersonal materialistic world, when we read these words, isn't it heart-warming to know that there is someone who is fascinated with what goes on in our lives, even though he may never gain anything from it?

Keep in mind what your romance partner has told you in his e-mail messages and in your chat sessions and ask questions on it as a follow-up. Show that you care and are interested. Don't assume that you know everything that is happening in the life of your romance partner. Always show that you are concerned.

How can you show that you are interested?

16. Toss in humour

Everyone likes a good laugh now and then, either to laugh at themselves or to laugh at others. Share a joke with your romance partner. Something funny that happened to you would be very welcome. It would show that you have the ability to laugh at yourself. Your aim, however, would be to put a smile on the face of the other.

With fun and laughter you would be able to enjoy a more relaxed atmosphere where you could flirt and have good clean fun. However, if you think you are not good at telling jokes, then you can do a web search for jokes and comical situations.

There are many web pages and websites where you can find jokes that will lighten a weary heart. Make sure you understand these jokes and their connotations first before you use these jokes in your communication with your romance partner. Don't assume that because they are jokes, they will be enjoyed. They could be misunderstood and their meaning misinterpreted.

What are the ways in which you could make your communication more humourous?

17. Be considerate

Consideration for your romance partner is not easy to show online. But there are subtle ways where you can display it. When writing to your romance partner who is in a different time zone, try to find out the difference in times. Make a note of it in the e-mail messages whenever you are mentioning your time. It will show that you are considerate enough to want the other to know the difference in times.

On other occasions, if you have been chatting with your romance partner for two hours (or more), enquire whether she is tired and want to call it a night. It is the simple gestures that are the most endearing.

Do you show consideration whenever you communicate online?

There are many more ingredients that you could add to spice up your online romance. You could add them to the ingredients already mentioned here.

CHAPTER 5

WORDS! WORDS! WORDS!

The choice of words in any form of communication, whether written or spoken, is crucial to the progress of any relationship.

It is said that words can ....
..... cause pain or happiness
..... crush a heart or give great joy
..... alienate a friend or make a friendship blossom
..... cause someone to go astray or help them find their way again
..... destroy someone's hopes and dreams or give a person reason to
       hope and dream again
..... make someone cry or take their tears away
..... make someone's day sad and dreary or make it happy and cheery
..... cause dark clouds to appear or bring back brighter days.

Words can either build or destroy. In your online romance then, your choice of words should help create a sense of caring that will lead to nurturing the romantic feeling between the two of you.

If one party does not initiate romance by flirting through the printed word in the e-mail or the chat, the relationship may carry on as a friendship forever. It is the words that will connect you to the loving mind and personality – the inner beauty - of your romance partner.

To begin flirting then, learn to express loving feelings in words which sound genuine, sincere and interesting. In an online romance, with the absence of the physical, you are challenged to try to fuel the imagination and influence your romance partner with loving words every time you communicate in the e-mail messages and chat sessions.

You will therefore have to be more sensitive and learn how to say the right words to comfort, soothe, calm, ease and help the other through the day. Because of the care and concern that you show, your romance partner will be more inclined to share intimate moments with you.

At the same time, you should encourage your romance partner to express his feelings in words. The mutual sharing of loving feelings will help create a bond. The extent to which romance and flirting goes requires the consent of both parties and it is a situation that has to be handled delicately, so be sensitive to your prospective romance mate. Thread carefully with your words.

Be considerate and get to know your romance partner a little before proceeding in your quest for romance. If your romance partner is not interested in sharing feelings and does not reciprocate your advances, then the flirting will be but in vain. An invitation like, "Want to talk dirty?", in one of your first few online encounters may result in you being deleted from her list of contacts.

If you do not know where to start and how to flirt with words, listen to sentimental songs. Pay attention to the lyrics in these songs. Pick the words and phrases that suit your purposes. Take a look at the following e-mail message and see if you can spot the titles of the songs that they come from.

> You're my everything. I am on top of the world when there is a message from you. I love you tenderly and deeply. What can I do to make you love me in return?

If you are too shy and do not know how your advances will be taken, a bit of humour will help. With a vivid imagination, you could write,

> I would like to give you a hug and a kiss but if you think that it is inappropriate, you can kick me in the shin with your high-heeled shoes.

Of course, you will not feel any pain because the kick is only given virtually. It will, however, definitely put a smile on your romance partner's face and draw her to you.

Words are a very powerful medium of expression. You can use them to convey your thoughts discreetly and subtly or directly and openly. For example, if your birthday is coming up and you know that your romance partner is not going to remember it, there are many ways for you to drop hints of what you would like for your birthday. So as not to be disappointed on your special day, be thick-skinned, and start a countdown to your birthday in every daily message.

But if you find that you do not have a way with words, just be human, expressing yourself in the same way you would be treating any other human being. By being human, it means that you have to be courteous and kind. Do not be condescending, talking down to your romance partner and belittling every little thing that he is doing. That is a sure way of ending the relationship.

You have to realise that not everyone acts and thinks like you. We have all been brought up differently and come from different backgrounds. Thus each of us is a unique entity. We should therefore learn to accept the differences, especially in the way of expression of ideas in words.

Do not nitpick. In e-mailing and chatting, what jumps out of a page of text is normally the spelling of words and the expression of ideas. So if your romance partner spells the word situation as 'situvation', and makes other atrocious blunders in spelling, just ignore them and accept his weakness. Nobody is perfect! Remember that you have your flaws, too. And it is the message and feelings behind the words that are more important. You have to compromise.

Be appreciative of every small little gesture, even the fact that your romance partner spent two hours chatting with you the previous night until you now have panda eyes because of lack of sleep. Instead of saying, "You kept me up until the wee hours of the morning in the chat room last night.", you could say, "I enjoyed every moment that I spent with you last evening. When can we do it again?"

The former sounds as though you are blaming him while the latter shows your appreciation. In fact, it would be nice if you could send a message of thanks after each chat session, thanking him for spending time with you. This small little gesture can be very touching.

You could also try to make the words sexier so that they invoke some romantic illusions in your romance partner when writing your e-mail messages and during your chat sessions. For example, you could address your romance mate as 'My Darrrling' and say that he makes you 'feel sooooo wonderful.'

Hold back on criticism. What is normally the outcome of any critical remark? And who likes to be criticised? It will only spoil the beautiful friendship that you have with your romance partner. On the contrary, always be positive and optimistic, passing remarks that will help the other person boost his self-esteem.

Say, "You sound so cheerful." rather than "Why are you so happy?". Since this comment is text that is read rather than something that is heard, the latter could seem as though you are accusing him and he does not deserve happiness.

From all the examples given, you will notice that in an online romance, because you are communicating through the printed word, the words play a very important role. You will not know the tone of voice that accompanies the words that are written. A simple reply like "No way!" can sound very rude to a simple request like "Shall we chat?". Courtesy should always be observed.

A smile, a gentle touch and a word of encouragement do go a long way to make another person feel great about himself and want to spend more time with you. Put these into words in your online romance. And always remember to express your feelings verbally, whether good or bad.

Decide which of the following comments invoke positive feelings in you and which do the opposite.

"I really want you to be happy."

"I wish you could have been there with me."

"I am fed up with this relationship. It seems to be going nowhere."

"Why am I always the one contacting you?"

"I wish I could kiss all your troubles away?"

"I notice that you contact me only when you have nothing else better to do."

Where words seem insufficient, you can make use of emoticons, abbreviations and lingo.

1) **Emoticons** convey emotions.

Emoticons are used in both e-mail messages and chat sessions. They range from a simple smile ☺ to even a flower @>-->--.

You could also be creative and come up with your own emoticons. Some original examples are shown below:

|| - a hug,

// - leaning too much on the other and so it could be typed in in either direction \\

~~ - sleeping in each other's arms or hugging each other while lying down.

2) **Abbreviations** have resulted from the common use of words and phrases by the general public. People who chat often on the Net have their own list of abbreviations.

You can use abbreviations in your chat sessions or e-mail messages when you feel that you have used the word or phrase so often with your romance partner that you do not want to spell out the whole word or phrase.

Some examples would be

C U L8er   – See you later
BF   – boyfriend
bf   – breakfast
AD   – annual dinner

3) **Lingo** is used to show action.

This is more commonly used in chat sessions than in e-mail messages. You use them to give your chat partner an idea of what you are doing or what you would like to do. Lingo is words typed in in response to what your chat partner would have written. It normally appears between two asterisks (*) or two tildes(~).

For example, if your chat partner has just told you a joke, you could then type in:

grin   or   ~grin~

to show that you find it funny. If you were angry with something your chat partner had mentioned, you could type in:

kick in the butt   or   ~kick in the butt~

Most e-mail programmes and chatrooms already have lists of emoticons, abbreviations and lingo. All you need to do is click on them to enhance your message. There are also many web pages which have these items listed. You could print them out and use them as appropriate.

If you are creative and innovative enough to come up with your own, do not hesitate to do so. It will be special and unique because it will be used only by the two of you. To avoid misinterpretation, explain to your romance partner what they mean the first time they are used.

Whenever you communicate with your romance partner, the words used must be constructive, making the romance partner feel like doing great things with himself. If words are not well used, it can destroy a person because it makes them feel useless and good-for-nothing. You could use flowery language or resort to the plain Jane style.

For example, if your romance partner has not sent you an e-mail message for the day, your complaint could go this way:
"Where is my daily dose of love to perk up my day?"
or you could just say (Plain Jane style),
"Why didn't you write?"

Here the use of emoticons would come in handy. "Why didn't you write?" sounds a bit demanding but with a sad face after that question, like this:
"Why didn't you write? ☹"
it shows that you are disappointed that there is no message from your romance partner.

Yes, there are a myriad ways to carry a message across with ordinary text, aided by emoticons, abbreviations and lingo. The more you communicate online, the better you will be at conveying your message effectively.

CHAPTER 6

THE UNWRITTEN

Using the right words at the appropriate time is very important to carry out the flirting with your romance partner online. To achieve your goal, the words chosen should show consideration and sensitivity that are endearing. The words should also evoke empathy and sincerity. The emoticons, abbreviations and lingo can help give a clearer picture of the tone of the message, so that it is not misinterpreted.

However, sometimes even if all these details are adhered to, they may not be enough to stir up romantic feelings in your romance partner. Wouldn't it be lovely if your romance partner said, "I got a toiletry kit for you when I was away on holiday recently." and a few days later the postman brings a parcel to your doorstep with the toiletry kit in it?

Very often, it is the words that are not said that draw us to another. Everyone wants to be thought of in a special way, especially by someone whom they feel for. So think of ways that will make your romance partner feel loved. Even if you are thousands of miles away, you can do that. How? There are many ways.

If, for example, you know that your romance partner has gone for a holiday, have a 'Welcome back' message waiting for him when he opens his In-box. If you knew that your romance partner was planning to attend an important interview, find out the time of the interview and send a message just before the interview. Send another message a couple of hours later to find out how it went.

Try to remember everything that your romance partner has told you, especially the nitty-gritty details. This can help strengthen the relationship. No matter how insignificant it is to you, it must have been something important in her life if she has shared it with you.

For example, if she has got a new job, at least know what her designation is. Taking on new jobs are always significant milestones in a person's life so if you keep on asking "So who are you working for again and what do you do?" your romance partner will get the message that you are not really interested in her as a person, and thus she would not be willing to comply with the flirting.

You cannot waltz into the heart of someone. It takes effort to secure a place there. Through the unwritten word, you could show that you want the privilege of being in that special place by the attention that you give that special someone. It could be a daily early morning message or even a virtual bouquet of roses now and then.

Saying "I love you" or "I care for you a lot" a thousand times without little concern for your romance partner and what is happening in her life will not get you very far in the world of romance. As they say, actions speak louder than words, so you should think of ways to make your romance partner more important than you, not only with the words that you use but how and when you use them.

CHAPTER 7

THE EXTRA MILE

How would you go that extra mile to make your message clear that you are interested romantically in your online friend and want to add a little spice to the relationship by flirting?

E-mailing and chatting are not the only means to communicate with your romance partner. Take advantage of the progress made in modern technology. There is always the phone where you could hear your romance partner's voice. You could even plan to have a Netmeeting. You could also install a webcam so that you could see each other while you are chatting. Snail mail could help you send photos and even presents to your heartthrob.

Make the relationship with your romance partner a priority if you want it to grow. The important thing is to spend time together by doing things together. Wanting to spend time together shows that you care for your romance partner and enjoy each other's company. There are lots of things that you can do together while online: play games, visit sites, and discuss current issues or even historical events. The list is endless.

For the fun of it, you could visit websites where you could take the following tests: a compatibility test or even a good kisser test. There are also tests online to find out what kind of lover you are and how passionate you can be. Discuss your findings with each other so that you will learn more about each other. This could also be the testing ground to see if you have mutual intentions where a romance is concerned.

You could also recall the times that you have shared and how it has made you feel. Talk about these spectacular moments often to indicate that you cherish them. Find some little incident which you could use to compliment your romance partner. Share it to make you both feel closer to each other. If you keep silent, your romance partner would never know how you feel, and may himself be too shy to let you know how he feels.

Not being able to see the other's face gives one the courage to be bold to send countless e-mail messages and initiate chat sessions. So be bold and try ways and means to get your heart's desire. There is no limit to the number of messages that you can send each day. There is also no limit to the length of the messages and what you say in those messages. Remember faint heart never won fair lady, so be persistent.

The key word in an online relationship is FEEL. Share boldly your feelings. Many people have succeeded in making their romance partner feel so valued that they have enticed them to leave husband, wife, children, family members and other loved ones, career, home and country to fly thousands of miles away to be with the virtual friend that they had spent hours online with - their soulmate.

In the long run, the online romance is much easier to manipulate because it does not matter how you look, speak or act in public. What matters is how you make only one person FEEL in private.

CHAPTER 8

THE OBSTACLES

What could go wrong in an online relationship? Everything and anything could go wrong, but not nothing. That is the reality. As in all relationships, something will definitely go wrong some time.

There will be hitches along the way. Family matters may take precedence. Sometimes it could be work commitments and other personal setbacks and problems. Even technology can work against the relationship. The network connection may get cut and it may be difficult to log back into the chat room. There are days on end when the computers are in the repair-room or being upgraded. He may not respond to your messages for awhile and then you will assume the worst: that he has ended the relationship, has found someone else or has died.

In this modern day and age, it is not uncommon to hear of fraud, scams and tricksters. The words in the e-mail messages and chat sessions could have been well chosen to entice the romance partner with a flawless picture. We have to be wary of such schemes.

Evaluate the relationship from time to time and everything that your romance partner has told you. Do not accept everything that is told as the gospel truth, especially since, even we sometimes tend to paint a better picture of ourselves.

Be aware of the risks involved in the online romance. To speculate whether your romance partner is truthful, ask questions in different ways about situations encountered. Analyse the answers. Do the stories always match? Are there loopholes that do not seem to add up but lead to more confusion and more questions?

If everything is going well with the online romance, you may come to a stage where your romance partner proposes. What should you do? You have to be very sure before you allow your heart to be smitten by someone you have never seen. Be realistic. This is a choice that you make on your own free will.

Not everyone would take this road of wanting to make a commitment with an online romance partner, but you could if you wanted to take the online romance to the next level of the relationship. Meet the person face-to-face before making a firm commitment. The real life relationship will not be the same as the one you are having online. The latter may be more exciting.

There are no guarantees in any relationship. Every relationship has its ups and downs. All relationships are a risk and there is no such thing as a perfect couple. Today, many seemingly stable real-life relationships have ended in divorce, separation and disunity in the family.

Even after thirty years (or more) of marriage, there are couples who drift apart. Because of the passing of time, people find that they are living in separate worlds, although they may be staying under the same roof. What has been lacking is communication.

What more in an online relationship where you never come in physical contact? There will be more chances for romance partners to go separate ways. To keep the romance, you will have to work extra harder. Always make sure that there is communication. Make allowances for the lack of attention or the shorter messages you are receiving.

Misunderstandings are bound to happen. These can be re-examined if the relationship is worth it. Discuss them in the open. You may have unconsciously projected your own expectations, anxieties and fears and this could have frightened your romance partner off.

Remember especially the differences in cultures. Being of a different culture and having different traditions, however, should not be a hindrance to the relationship. On the contrary, it should only be a force that strengthens the relationship further because it is in our diversity that we sometimes find beauty and the unexpected.

You could share with each other stories that are popular in your culture. Customs and traditions when discussed give us a better understanding of our values and a sense of pride in our heritage. If we are open-minded, we will undoubtedly learn a lot, not only about ourselves but about the world we live in.

For example, most people would know what a barbecue is, but very few know about a steamboat meal. No, it is not having a meal in a boat but steamboat is cooking bite pieces of food like fish, prawns, meat and vegetables in a small boat-shaped pan filled with soup on the dining table. It is part of Chinese cuisine. Sharing culture, customs and traditions makes us realise what a wonderful world of diversity we live in.

Having an online friend could also take you away from the real world. It has made some people neglect their household chores and work commitments. So although you have an online romance in tow, you will still need to build relationships around you in the real world. Do not get too caught up with your romance online that you cannot decide what is real and what is not. Although you are in the virtual world of romance, keep your feet on terra firma.

Your romance partner will not be the same today as he was years ago when you met. Success or failure may have come his way. You yourself may have faced disappointments or accolades in family and career. Accept the fact that the two of you may change because of circumstances beyond your control.

Since the relationship involves both parties, discuss it often. Talk about what you are not satisfied with and what you want to see improved. Make your complaints verbally. Don't suffer in silence. Ask for clarifications in your e-mail and your chat sessions, but do not overdo it. By talking through your problems, you will find that you will be preventing issues from developing into bigger problems, which may be more difficult to solve later.

If each party is sensitive enough, he will know that the complaints are only a sign of care and concern for the progress and development of the relationship. An even more mature loving relationship may form as a result of the boat being on the rocks for awhile. If he ignores the complaints and the situation persists, it is time for a change.

If you only experience heartache and there is no mutual sharing, it is time to go separate ways. It is no point holding on to something that is not there anymore. Delete all the messages from your In-box. Cancel off his name from your address list.

Unfortunately, it is much easier said than done!

CHAPTER 9

MARS AND VENUS

Do men view relationships in the same way that women do? There are many differences between men and women. Physically and psychologically each gender is different. Thus, each thinks, feels and acts in different ways.

Men are emotionally more aggressive. They tend to be more individualistic, feeling closer to others only because of mutual activities participated in. That is why many men like to become members of clubs and associations. They rely on rational thought and remember tasks or activities.

Generally, women are more nurturing. They are more social and feel closeness towards others through the communication of experiences, dialogue and sharing. They rely on feelings and personal perspectives. They base their information about events or experiences on emotion and how they felt at the time.

Even intellectually, men and women are different. Each gender approaches situations with different mentalities. Women are said to have four times as many brain cells connecting the right and left side of the brain. That is why when men rely on their left brain to solve one problem at a time, women can solve more than one problem at the same time since they have greater access to both sides of their brains.

Despite the differences, or is it because of the differences, men and women find each other attractive. They are drawn to each other and complement each other. In a machine, because the grooves and teeth of the gears oppose each other, the machine works. This also happens in a relationship between a man and a woman.

No two human beings are alike and neither can we generalise that all men are made in one way and all women are made in another. What we have to realise is that there are differences between the male and the female gender. We have to accept the differences and compromise wherever possible. We should understand and appreciate our romance partners for the persons they are, flaws and all.

But this does not mean that you have to sacrifice everything for your romance partner. You have to believe in your own individuality and not be bullied into thinking that you have to do everything that your romance partner desires. If you are unhappy in the relationship, call it quits!

Any relationship should be one that helps you to grow and inspires you to make the world a better place for the people around you. If you find yourself doing good for B because A has treated you well, then carry on that relationship with A. If not, then it is time for a change.

CHAPTER 10

WHEN THINGS DON'T WORK OUT

What happens when the messages stop and there are no more chat sessions? What happens when your potential romance partner does not want to share his feelings and time with you? Don't despair. Treat it as
- a learning experience,
- a means by which you got to know yourself better,
- a memorable time you had spent with someone special, someone who has made your life more meaningful by just being in it. Keep these precious memories in your heart.

While you had been together, you may have made a list of all his sterling qualities to convince yourself that the time you spent together online was not wasted. Now that the relationship has come to an end, make a list of all the issues that you were dissatisfied with while you were together. Don't be generous with praise. Console yourself that you put in a lot of effort and the break-up is not your fault.

Then when you have got over the hurt of him not returning your messages, move on. This could take days for some, weeks for others and even years for a few. But move on, you must! Always look at life this way: You have only one life so you should make the most of it. The break-up has opened the door to a chance of an even better relationship with someone more exciting!

There will definitely be more exciting people to get to know online. Statistics show that there were 670 million Net users in the world in 2003. The breakdown of Net users was as follows:

Africa	-	8 million
America	-	229 million
Asia	-	209 million
Europe	-	196 million
Middle East	-	12 million
Oceania	-	14 million.

With so many people just a click away, there is sure to be someone out there who will be able to 'click' with you. You have to test the ground.

Is there a set plan or strategy? What is the modus operandi? Every relationship takes a different course because it involves two different human beings coming together. It will be up to you to decide which tips and tricks mentioned in this book work for you.

If you feel that you are not ready for a one-to-one relationship, join a romance group. Search the member directories of websites and if they have a romance group, fill out a member profile so that you can join them for chat sessions, discussions and forums. Some groups have 30 members, some have 30,000 members.

When you feel that you are ready or you think you have spotted someone interesting in the group, request for a one-to-one chat and take it from there. You will realise that despite your heartbreak after the break-up, the online romance prevails!

ABOUT THE AUTHOR

The author of "Secrets to a Successful Online Romance" who goes under the pen name of Jensel Darul has written and published many books in the academic arena. She has also given many lectures to students and adult learners on Communication Skills in her home country. This is her first attempt at writing a book concerning the affairs of the heart.

The idea of this book and the thoughts behind it are based on her own experiences of communicating with Net-users over the past five years, and successfully having an on-line romance of her own for the past four years. The latter relationship is still strong and she hopes to take it to a higher level some day soon.